Library of Congress Cataloging-in-Publication Data Available

2 4 6 8 10 9 7 5 3 1

Published by Sterling Publishing Co., Inc.
387 Park Avenue South, New York, NY 10016
Text copyright © 2006 by Harriet Ziefert
Illustrations copyright © 2006 by Jennifer Rapp
Distributed in Canada by Sterling Publishing
c/o Canadian Manda Group, 165 Dufferin Street,
Toronto, Ontario, Canada M6K 3H6
Distributed in Great Britain by GMC Distribution Services,
Castle Place, 166 High Street, Lewes, East Sussex, England BN7 1XU
Distributed in Australia by Capricorn Link (Australia) Pty. Ltd.
P.O. Box 704, Windsor, NSW 2756, Australia

Printed in China

Sterling ISBN-13: 978-1-4027-2671-2
ISBN-10: 1-4027-2671-6

For information about custom editions, special sales, premium and
corporate purchases, please contact Sterling Special Sales
Department at 800-805-5489 or specialsales@sterlingpub.com.

Pregnancy's Little Miseries

Harriet Ziefert

drawings by

Jennifer Rapp

Sterling Publishing Co., Inc.

New York

FIRST TRIMESTER

Misery is not knowing whether

you're pregnant or just gaining weight

and losing your waistline.

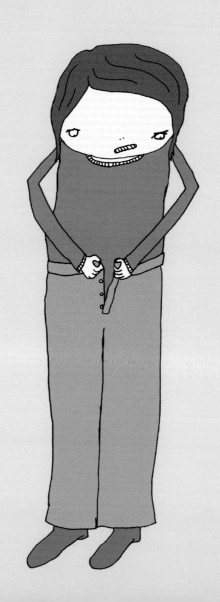

Misery is knowing

a pregnancy is nine months,

or forty weeks, but from what date

do you begin counting?

Misery is just wanting

to curl up and take a nap.

Dear Mr. Bojangles:

Per our conversation earlier today,
I will be putting together[q/a].

Misery is having PMS symptoms

for weeks and weeks.

Misery is when your breasts

hurt all the time.

Misery is morning sickness in the afternoon.

And in the evening, too.

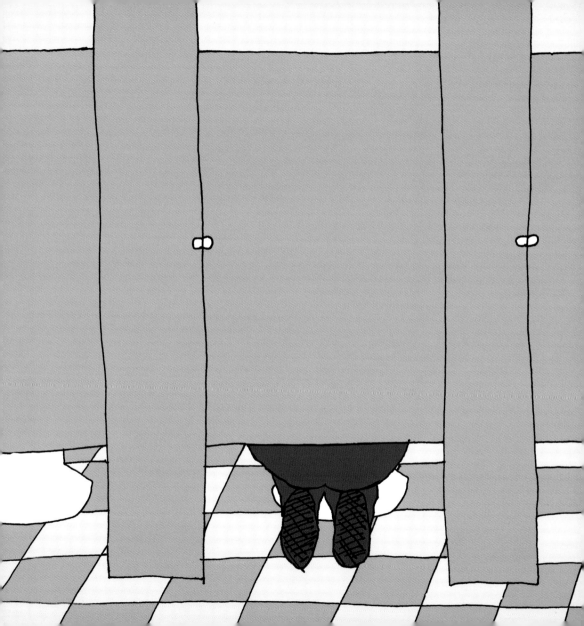

Misery is needing to pee
every hour.

Misery is switching to

pants with elastic waistbands.

Misery is craving

the most fattening foods.

Misery is being introduced to your baby,

who looks just like a lima bean.

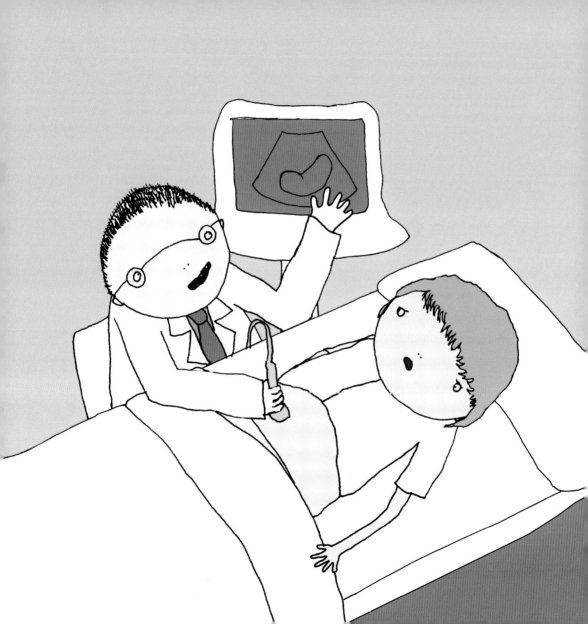

Misery is gaining ten pounds

in ten weeks.

Misery is waiting till the end of

the first trimester to share the good news:

"We're pregnant."

SECOND TRIMESTER

Misery is enduring a cold—

without medication.

Misery is suffering from

the unpleasant side effects—

constipation, belching, nausea, indigestion—

of your prenatal vitamin.

Misery is bad acne—

just like when you were a teenager.

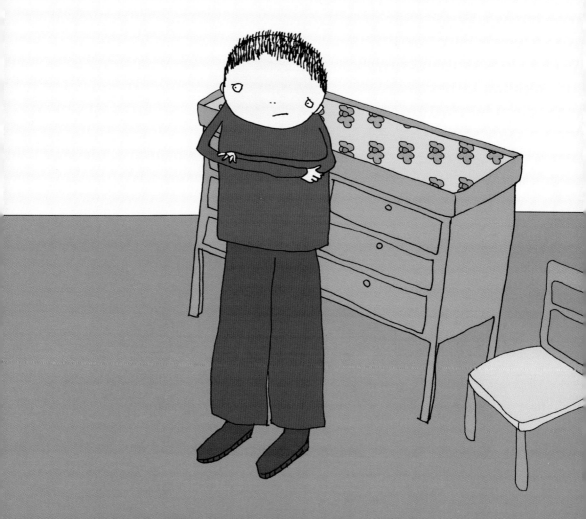

Misery is attempting to

create the "perfect" baby's room.

Misery is when nothing fits—

except your husband's shirts.

Misery is shopping for maternity clothes

with a friend who wears a size 4.

Misery is receiving "parenting" advice
from everyone—including your Aunt Tillie,
who's never had children.

Misery is gaining another ten pounds
and realizing that your baby still
weighs less than one pound.

Misery is strangers who think

your big belly gives them permission

to ask inappropriate questions.

THIRD TRIMESTER

Misery is an equally pregnant friend

whose belly is smaller than yours.

Misery is a perpetual backache

and frequent indigestion—instead of

the promised inner glow.

Misery is listening to at least
one labor-and-delivery
"horror" story every week.

Misery is an overanxious mother,

who repeats the details of your birth

every time you see her.

Misery is constant heartburn—

from even the blandest foods.

Misery is searching for

a baby's name that begins with "L":

Logan, Louie, Leslie, Lulu,

Lily, Lawrence . . .

Misery is the intrusive stranger

who feels free to pat your belly.

Misery is the person who says:

"Wow, you're really huge!"

when there are still six weeks

till your due date.

Misery is a partner
who says...

Misery is swollen ankles,

swollen feet, and swollen legs—

in addition to your swollen belly.

大ショック！
この時に赤ちゃんを守るために
お腹周りについたぜい肉は、
一度は元に戻りますが、やがては
永遠のぜい肉となって残ります。
妊娠期間の思い出として大事に
しましょう。

Misery is shopping for bigger bras—

for the third time!

Misery is being a bridesmaid

two weeks before your due date.

Misery is shortness of breath
and swollen feet.

男には、この気持わからない！

Misery is never finding

a comfortable sleeping position.

You are here!
後、もう少し、ガンバッテ！

Misery is trying to concentrate

when you really want to be

at home "nesting."

Misery is waiting impatiently
while your doctor is at the hospital
delivering someone else's baby.

Misery is the doctor who says,

"See you next week,"

and makes an appointment two days

after your due date.

Misery is a labor that starts
at midnight and continues through
much of the following day.

分娩台に上がったら、落ち着いて
ラマーズ法の呼吸を思い出して・・・
な〜んて言ってるどころの騒ぎでは
ありません。
後は、運を天に任せて、自然の
リズムをつかみながら『母は強し』で
産み切るのみ！
お腹の赤ちゃんも懸命にこの世に
出て来ようとしていることを、
どうかお忘れなく！

And happiness is

a healthy, beautiful baby . . .

母親になったということを
心から実感できる瞬間
幸せ〜

The Most Memorable Moment!!!
Blessings!

who cries only

25 percent of each day!

母乳が出れば、胸がますます豊かになり
それだけでも幸せです。
で〜も、その後は、ヒ・ミ・ツ・・・

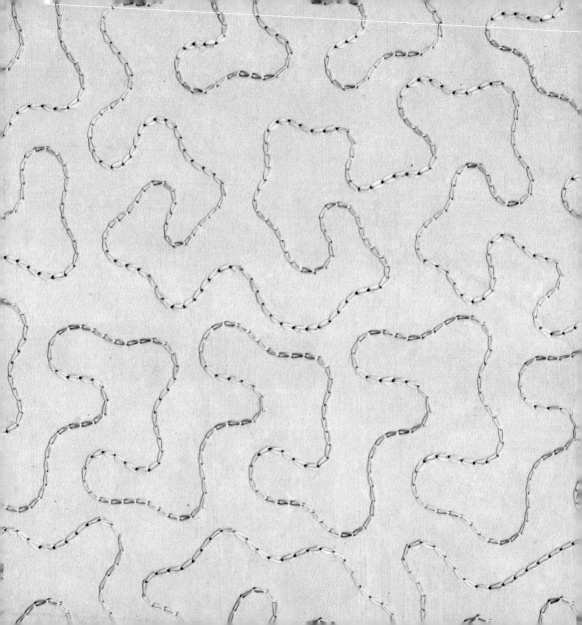